MARKETING COPYWRITING
Learn the art of writing great marketing copy

Copyright

Copyright © 2021 by Njoku Caleb - All rights reserved.

No part of this book may be reproduced, stored in a retrieval system, or transmitted in any form or by any means, without the prior written permission of the publisher, except in the case of brief quotations embedded in critical articles or reviews.

Every effort has been made in the preparation of this book to ensure the accuracy of the information presented. However, the information contained in this book is sold without warranty, either express or implied. Neither the author nor its dealers or distributors will be held liable for any damages caused or alleged to be caused directly or indirectly by this book.

All trademarks and brands within this book are for clarifying purposes only and are the owned by the owners themselves, not affiliated with this document.

Dedication

This guide is dedicated to every marketer who is aspiring to improve and horn his/her marketing skill.

Table of Contents

Copyright 2
Dedication 3
Introduction 3
Nine Qualities of Good Writing 4
Add These Five Word 'Magnets' to Your Marketing and Sales Vocabulary 9
    Selling Is a Process… and Words Are a Powerful Part of That Process 9
    Marketing Magnets 10
        The First Marketing Magnet: 'New' or 'Exclusive' 11
        The Second Marketing Magnet: 'Fast' 12
        The Third Marketing Magnet: 'Quick' 12
        The Fourth Marketing Magnet: 'Easy' 12
        The Fifth Marketing Magnet: 'Guarantee' 13
    Parting Words 14
The Epic Face-Off in Copywriting: Hype vs. No-Hype 15
Three Deceptively Simple (but Powerful) Tips for Writing Persuasive Landing Page Copy 17
    1. Every element on your landing page has one job 18
    2. Always start with the page goal and work backwards 19
    3. Stop trying to write 20
    Here's the bottom line 21
Five Content Writing Tips That Will 22
Automatically Make You a Better Blogger 22
    1. Use the AIDA formula 22
    2. Don't write for search engines 23
    3. Use the word 'you' 23
    4. Be conversational 23

- 5. Use the KISS principle 24

The Benefits of Byline Authorship, and How to Do It Right 25
- Write articles that humans would want to read 25
- Craft a compelling pitch and target it to the right publication 27
- Distribute your published article and encourage readers to share it via social media 28

Lessons From the Greatest Marketer of All Time...Expelled From Oxford 29
- The Wilderness Years 29
- Founding an Agency 29
- Five of Ogilvy's Most Important Marketing Lessons 30

Writing and Readability Scores: It Matters 33
- Some Best-Practices for Writing for the Web 33
- Flesch-Kincaid Readability Scoring 34
- Determining Readability in MS Word 37
- Troubleshooting 38

Five Incredibly Specific Tactics for Writing Enchanting Copy 40
- 1. Branded statements 40
- 2. Use fragments 41
- 3. Show vulnerability 42
- 4. Steal words 43
- 5. Get visual 44

Five Tips to Enhance Your Call to Action 46
- 1. Use a Widget 46
- 2. Offer Prizes 46
- 3. Personalization 47
- 4. Clarity of Intent 47
- 5. Repetition 48

Five Surprising Ways to Write Addictive Business Blog Posts 49

1. Write with all five senses 49

2. Get to the point 50

3. Ignore your English teacher 50

4. Embarrass yourself 51

5. Don't be a show-off 52

Give your readers their fix 52

This Writing GPS Helps You Create Ridiculously Good Content 54

1. Goal. 55

2. Reframe. 55

3. Seek out the data and examples. 56

4. Organize. 57

5. Write to one person. 57

6. Produce The Ugly First Draft. 58

7. Walk away. 58

8. Rewrite. 58

9. Give it a great headline or title. 59

10. Have someone edit. 59

11. One final look for readability. 59

12. Publish 59

Introduction

Copywriting is the art of writing text for marketing purposes. It's designed to sell your products or services while establishing a voice for your brand.

If you have a web site, you are a publisher. If you are on social media, you are in marketing. And that means that we are all relying on our words to carry our marketing messages.

The main intention of copywriting is to persuade people to take a particular action, whether it's purchasing, signing up for something, or any other type of conversion. Copywriting is much more than just words. Great copy tells a compelling story and represents your brand image. It pulls on the strings that trigger the decision-making process for whoever reads what you're writing.

In our content-driven marketing world, being able to communicate well in writing isn't just nice; it's a necessity. And yet writing is the oft-overlooked cornerstone of nearly all our content marketing.

We hope this guide will give you both inspiration and instruction you need to strengthen your own writing chops. Because writing matters more now, not less.

P.S. At the end of this guide, you'll find my 12-step writing GPS. It provides step-by-step directions for writing your next piece of content. Print it out and use it when you've got an assignment due!

Nine Qualities of Good Writing

There are two kinds of people when it comes to writing: Those who think they can write, and those who think they can't. And, very often, both are wrong.

The truth is, most of us fall somewhere in the middle. We are all capable of producing good writing. Or, at least, *better* writing.

Why does good writing matter? Isn't the best content marketing very often something short, snappy, and non-text? Like Skype's Born Friends video, Lowe's Vines, or Chipotle's haunting video commentary?

Sometimes, yes. But here I'm not just talking about content in a marketing context. I'm talking about content, *period*.

Text is the backbone of the Web, and it's often the backbone of any content you watch or listen to, as well. That Born Friends video started with a story and a script.

Words matters. Your words (what you say) and style (how you say it) are your most cherished (and undervalued) assets.

Yet, so often, they are overlooked. Think of it this way: If a visitor came to your website without its branding in place (logo, tagline, and so on), would he or she recognize it as yours? Are you telling your story there from your unique perspective, with a voice and style that's clearly all you?

Here, in no particular order, is what I've learned about the necessary qualities of good writing (or content, in our digital vernacular), based on my many years of working as a writer and editor... and even longer career as a reader.

1. Good writing anticipates reader questions.

Good writing serves the reader, not the writer. It isn't indulgent. "The reader doesn't turn the page because of a hunger to applaud," said long time writing teacher Don Murray. Rather, good writing anticipates what questions readers will have as they read a piece, and (before they ask them) it answers them.

That means most good writers are natural skeptics, especially regarding their own work. They relentlessly think of things from their reader's point of view: *What experience is this creating for the reader? What questions might they have?*

(I did this above, when, before listing the qualities of good writing, I thought, "Why does good writing even matter to you? Why should any of us care?")

George Orwell said the "scrupulous writer" will ask himself at least four questions in every sentence: *"What am I trying to say? What words will express it? What image or idiom will make it clearer? Is this image fresh enough to have an effect?* And he or she will probably ask himself two more: *Could I put it more shortly? Have I said anything that is avoidably ugly?"*.

Here's where marketing can really help add value in a business context, by the way, because "simple" means "making it easy for the customer." It means being the
advocate for them. As Georgy Cohen writes, "The marketer should be identifying (and ruthlessly refining) the core messages and the top goals, then working with the web professionals to create a website supporting them."

2. Good writing is grounded in data.
Data puts your content in context and gives you credibility. Ground your content in facts: Data, research, fact-checking and curating. Your ideas and opinions and spin might be part of that story—or they might not be, depending on what you are trying to convey. But content that's rooted in something true—not just your own opinions—is more credible.

Said another way: Data before declaration. If you are going to tell me what you think, give me a solid reason why you think it.

3.   Good writing is like good teaching.
Good writing strives to explain, to make things a little bit clearer, to make sense of our world… even if it's just a product description.

"A writer always tries… to be part of the solution, to understand a little about life and to pass this on," says Anne Lamott in Bird by Bird.

4. Good writing tells a full story.

Good writing roots out opposing viewpoints. As Joe Chernov says, "There's a name for something with a single point of view: It's called a press release." Incorporate multiple perspectives when the issue lends itself to that. At the very least, don't ignore the fact that other points of view might exist; to do so makes your reader not trust you.

So make sure he or she knows you're watching out for them. To quote Hemingway: "The most essential gift for a good writer is a built-in, shockproof, shit detector."

5. Good writing comes on the rewrite.

That implies that there *is* a rewrite, of course. And there should be.

Writing is hard work, and producing a shitty first draft is often depressing. But the important thing is to get something down to start chipping into something that resembles a coherent narrative.

As Don Murray said, "The draft needs fixing, but first it needs writing." Or Mark Twain: "Writing is easy. All you have to do is cross out the wrong words."

6. Good writing is like math.

I mean this in two ways: First, good writing has logic and structure. It feels solid to the reader: The writer is in control and has taken on the heavy burden of shaping a lumpy jumble of thoughts into something clear and accessible.

It might not follow a formula, exactly. But there's a kind of architecture to it. Good writing has more logic to it than you might think.

> Second, good writing is inherently teachable—just as trigonometry or algebra or balancing a balance sheet is a skill any of us can master. Journalism professor Matt Waite writes in his essay, How I Faced My Fears and Learned to Be Good at Math: "The difference between good at math and bad at math is hard work. It's trying. It's trying hard. It's trying harder than you've ever tried before. That's it."

I think the same is true about writing. Ta-Nehisi Coates, a senior editor at *The Atlantic*, spent a year teaching writing to MIT students. He later wrote, "I felt that the rigor of math had better prepared these kids for the rigor of writing. One of my students insisted that whereas in math you could practice and get better, in writing you either 'had it' or you didn't. I told her that writing was more like math then she suspected."

7. Good writing is simple, but not simplistic.

Business—like life—can be complicated. Products can be involved or concepts may seem impenetrable. But good content deconstructs the complex to make it easily understood: It sheds the corporate Frankenspeak and conveys things in human, accessible terms. A bit of wisdom from my journalism days: *No one will ever complain that you've made things too simple to understand.*

"Simple" does not equal "dumbed-down." Another gem from my journalism professors: *Assume the reader knows nothing. But don't assume the reader is stupid.*

If you think your business-to-business concept is too complex to be conveyed simply, take a look at the very first line of The Economist's style guide: "The first requirement of *The Economist* is that it should be readily understandable. Clarity of writing usually follows clarity of thought. So think what you want to say, then say it as simply as possible."

8. Good writing doesn't get hung up on what's been said before.

Rather, it elects to simply say it better. Here's where style becomes a differentiator—in literature and on your website.

Mark Twain described how a good writer treats sentences: "At times he may indulge himself with a long one, but he will make sure there are no folds in it, no vaguenesses, no parenthetical interruptions of its view as a whole; when he has done with it, it won't be a sea-serpent with half of its arches under the water; it will be a torch-light procession." He also might've said: "Write with clarity and don't be indulgent." But he didn't.

That doesn't mean you need to be a literary genius, of course. It only means you have to hone your own unique perspective and voice.

7. A word about writers: Good writers aren't smug.

Most of the really good writers I know still feel a little sheepish calling themselves a "writer," because that's a term freighted with thick tomes of excellence. But like many achievements in life—being called a success, or a good parent—the label seems more meaningful when it's bestowed upon you by others.

"Most of the time I feel stupid, insensitive, mediocre, talentless and vulnerable—like I'm about to cry any second—and wrong. I've found that when that happens, it usually means I'm writing pretty well, pretty deeply, pretty rawly." —Andre Dubus III (House of Sand and Fog)

BONUS
Good writing has a good editor. Writers get the by-line and any glory. But behind the scenes, a good editor adds a lot to process.

Remember what I said above about there being two kinds of people? Those who think they can write, and those who think they can't? And very often, both being wrong? A good editor teases the best out of so-called writers and non-writers alike.

The best writing—like the best parts of life, perhaps— is collaborative.

And by the way, is it odd that I'm seeding what's essentially business advice with insight from artists? And if so, why is that odd?

Because in a world where we have an opportunity and responsibility to tell our stories online, we need to find not just the right words... but the very best ones.

Add These Five Word 'Magnets' to Your Marketing and Sales Vocabulary

This article is based on an excerpt from the book Life's a Pitch: Understanding the Secrets to Selling From Television's Billion Dollar Man.

Words. They can be powerful, passionate, and—when used correctly in marketing and sales communications and presentations—extremely profitable.

Have you ever wondered why some of the same "power words" keep showing up in advertising messages year after year?

- "Act Now!"
- "Limited Time Only!"
- "Money Back Guarantee!"
- "Time's Running Out!"
- "Six Brand New Features!"
- And so on...

The fact is, words are a powerful part of marketing and selling.

Selling Is a Process... and Words Are a Powerful Part of That Process

It doesn't matter whether it's taking place on TV or in person, selling is a process composed of several layers, each designed to increase the connection between you and the customer.

For instance, when I'm pitching something on radio or television, every time I do something effective, people in the audience get a little closer to the telephone. And after each effective step of the process, they get closer and closer to that phone until they pick it up and respond. And that's natural. It's all part of a process.

I wish I could tell you that there's one magic word that will make somebody buy something. There isn't. But there are certain words that will enhance the process.

Seven of them, to be exact. Here, we present five of those word magnets.

Marketing Magnets

George Carlin gained instant notoriety back in the 70s with his "Seven Words You Can't Say on Television" bit. But there are seven words you CAN say to create an indelible connection with a potential customer? I call them my "Seven Marketing Magnets" because, as I explained a few moments ago, every time you use one of them—for the right reasons, at the right time—you draw people a little closer to you, like a magnet.

The connection becomes stronger, and the temptation to buy from you greater. Which is not to say that more is more in this case. In other words, don't just arbitrarily string these words together, piling them on or (for heaven's sake) using them randomly—or even interchangeably.

Each word is calculated to highlight the benefits of the particular product, service, or idea you're presenting. That is their power: Each means something very specific to whoever hears them.

Remember, the ultimate goal is a response. Hopefully, the response of a sale, but short of that the response might be in the form of interest, curiosity, enthusiasm, a personal connection with you, a renewed interest in what you're presenting, etc.

That's why these words are so effective: They evoke strong responses in your listeners, each in its own way.

The First Marketing Magnet: 'New' or 'Exclusive'

The first marketing magnet is "new," or "exclusive." Those are great words; I get excited just typing them... they're filled with so much potential. Now, either word could describe any of the following:

- A price you're offering: "Enjoy our *new*, reduced price for a limited time..."

- A special ingredient you're using: "Try our *new* combination of lime and pomegranate seed."

- A part of a service you're offering: "Enjoy our *exclusive* steam-cleaning solution..."

- A special online offer: "Download an extra chapter of this NEW bestseller *exclusively* on Amazon.com..."

- And so on...

That's a pretty impressive list, and you can of course personalize it for whatever "new" or "exclusive" features and benefits you're offering. But even powerful, profitable, magnetic words can become less effective when used nonstop. So don't just say, "New," "New," "Exclusive," "New," all the time. Spice your sales pitch up with the following other ways to say the same thing:

- Innovative

- The latest

- State of the art

- Revolutionary (use only when referring to a patented or patent-pending product)

- High-tech

- Designed for today's _____

- Adds a whole new dimension to _____

- Here's an exciting way to _____

- And so on…

The Second Marketing Magnet: 'Fast'

The Third Marketing Magnet: 'Quick'

The Fourth Marketing Magnet: 'Easy'

Our second, third, and fourth marketing magnets are the words "fast," "quick," and "easy." I combine them because they really share the same spirit—of modern convenience and benefits that really appeal to the way we live our lives today.

The Internet and other high technology have spoiled us so that we can't wait for anything anymore. We want it all, and we want it now… We want it fast, quick, and easy.

Now, these words can be used individually, of course, but I tend to lump them together when I'm making a presentation because they work so well in combination.

So, in this case, fast, quick, and easy could refer to…

- Results you want the customer to achieve: "Drying your hair has never been *faster* with our breakthrough technology!"

- The application of something: "The *fastest, quickest, easiest* way to wash your car, spot-free!"

- Pointing out a product feature: "With our age defying product, looking younger has never been *easier* or *quicker* than this!"

- Creating an added benefit: "With our product, you'll discover how *easy* it is to _____."

- After-purchase care: "Our platinum customer service is *fast*, *quick*, and *easy*, all day, every day."

- And so on...

Naturally, even three marketing magnets like "fast," "quick," and "easy" can get overplayed, so here are some handy alternatives that are equally effective:

- Step by step

- As easy as 1, 2, 3

- Immediate results

- Ready to use

- Wash and wear

- Set it and forget it

- And so on...

The Fifth Marketing Magnet: 'Guarantee'

Our fifth marketing magnet is one you hear quite often, particularly on late-night TV: "guarantee." As powerful as this word is, you have to be very, very careful when using it.

For instance, you just can't guarantee certain results, such as "With our foolproof system, you are guaranteed to make a million dollars, lose 50-pounds, look 12 years younger, etc."

However, there is one thing we can all guarantee: satisfaction. And we should all guarantee satisfaction with a money back, 30-day satisfaction guarantee—often called the "promise to please" in our industry.

When you're talking about your product, service, or idea, I want you to imagine a brick wall between you and the other person. Every time you minimize a risk, you are essentially taking off a row of bricks and moving that other person closer and closer to the results you want.

Minimize another risk, and one more row of bricks comes down until pretty soon there's nothing left between you and the other person. And that's the moment you create a true "win/win" situation.

That satisfaction, 30-day, money-back guarantee language really helps secure a fast and tight bond between you and the other person because it minimizes so much risk.

Parting Words

When used effectively, these five words will move you closer to what you're after: a strong response from your listener. They will help tear down the brick wall that stands between you and them at the beginning of your interaction, all the while helping to create a stronger, lasting relationship that will ultimately lead to sales.

And yes, I do guarantee that!

Three Deceptively Simple (but Powerful) Tips for Writing Persuasive Landing Page Copy

Does the following sound familiar?

You're struck with inspiration and you write *what you think* is killer landing page copy. All the essential elements are there: social proof, your unique value proposition, a detailed list of benefits, and a clear headline. You've also brushed up on your psychology to make your argument more persuasive, and you employ all the best-practices you know.

But then you check your analytics… and in spite of all your hard work, your conversion rate sucks.

What gives?

Writing a persuasive landing page isn't as simple as running through a checklist of best-practices.

To write landing page copy that converts like crazy, you need to take a step back and look at the larger picture: Are you creating **a seamless, engaging experience that is custom-tailored to your prospects' goals, pushing them closer to that precious conversion?**

In "The Conversion Marketer's Guide to Landing Page Copywriting," conversion-centered copywriter Joanna Wiebe shares the process she uses to engineer high-converting landing pages. Keep reading for three deceptively simple (but super powerful) tactics for writing landing page copy that converts.

1. Every element on your landing page has one job

Copywriters spend hours crafting the perfect headline for their landing page—and they have high expectations for the 6-12 words they choose.

For many, headlines are expected to convey the UVP, convince people to buy, summarize the offer, contain all the right SEO keywords… and more.

But Joanna calls BS on the belief that the headline should have that much responsibility. If you expect it to do everything—from summarizing your offer to sealing the deal—then you'll wind up with *a headline that is trying to be too much (and so fails)*.

Yes, of course it's still important, but, Joanna insists, your headline has one job, and one job only: **to keep those arriving visitors on the page**.

That's it. One job.

That logic extends to the rest of your landing page. In the e-book, Joanna explains that **every** landing page element **has only one job:**

Headline	Keep arriving visitors on the page
Subhead	Move visitors to the body copy
Body copy	Directly support the page goal
Social proof	Turn naysayers into believers
Form headline	Relieve anxiety about completing the page goal
Form	Get filled out
Button	Get clicked

When each of these elements is optimized for its unique role, you'll have created a clear, deliberate path for prospects, leading them toward your conversion goal. And *that makes your prospects' experience of your landing page seamless.*

Here's how Joanna puts it: "Think of the elements on your page as workers on an assembly line. Every worker has her own job for which she is responsible." Every job must be done well to keep the conveyor belt going; if one job along the line isn't done well, it makes it impossible for the other workers down the line to do their job well.

And once you understand the "one job" of each element, it's much easier to perfect the page as a whole. Running A/B tests to optimize your copy is simple when you know precisely what you're optimizing for.

2. Always start with the page goal and work backwards

Just as every page element has one job, Joanna explains, every landing page should have only one goal.

If you want prospects to download your latest whitepaper, they don't need to know about your upcoming webinar. And as awesome as your latest blog post is, you shouldn't be linking to it.

This all comes back to perfecting the attention ratio of your landing page: the ratio of *things you can do* to the *number of campaign conversion goals—which should always be one:*

Once you're clear on your one goal, here's what Joanna suggests you do next: "The goal is what matters. So start there, and **work backward through the sequence of objections and anxieties that are most likely to get in the way of conversion,** all the way up to the point where you've found the benefit or value prop to message in your headline."

Reverse-engineering your landing pages by starting with the goal allows you to ensure that every element you add is aligned with the action you want people to take. That creates a smooth, friction-free experience for your prospect—which pushes them to convert.

3. Stop trying to write

There's nothing more frustrating than toiling over landing page copy only to put it in front of your audience and find that you've completely missed the mark.

Instead of straining to come up with killer copy, take a step back: "When you stop trying to write and start listening to your customers, your copy writes itself."

Best-performing landing page copy is stolen straight from customers—whether from testimonials, customer reviews, support emails, surveys, forums, social media groups, or anywhere else prospects are talking about your solution (or that of your competitors).

"Stealing" your marketing messages from these channels is effective because you're **speaking the customer's language.**

By borrowing the terms they use when they're candidly describing their problem, you're sure to create messages that really resonate with others feeling the same pain.

Beyond "stealing" the customer's language from testimonials, you may also want to consider making your testimonials the star of your landing page.

Consider this landing page example from Freshdesk:

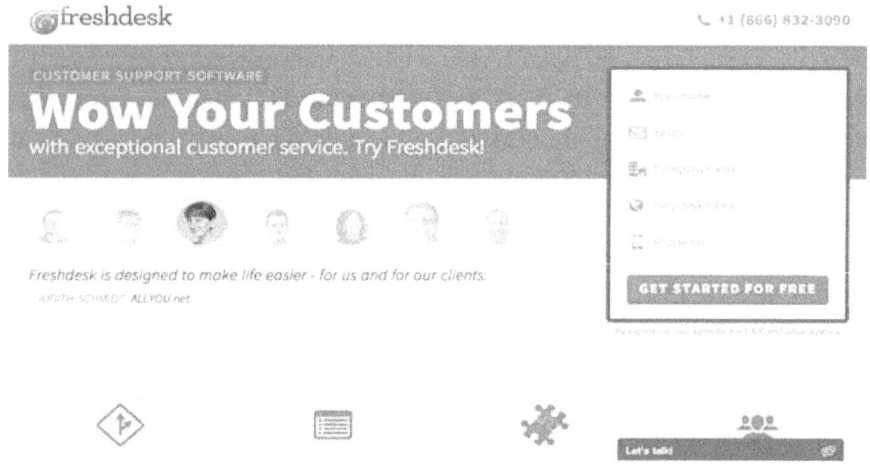

Successful testimonials can be exponentially more powerful than anything you could ever write yourself: "That testimonial is a marketing message—but it's far more powerful than regular marketing copy because **you're not the one saying it.** Your customer is. Your customer with a face and a name and a business."

If you want your testimonials to hit it out of the park, be sure that...

- They focus on *your customer's pain point*—not your product.

- They are phrased naturally and believably (even real testimonials can sound fake).

Here's the bottom line

It doesn't matter how valuable your offer is or how talented your designer is... If you can't write copy that resonates with your prospects, then your landing pages won't convert.

Here's how Joanna puts it: "If you listen to your prospects, write in their language, write toward the page goal—making it *their* goal—and let a little love into your copy, you could see incredible conversion lifts... using only your words."

Next time you set out to write landing page copy, put yourself in your prospect's shoes. Ask yourself *what* they need to hear from you in order to make a decision. Then ask yourself *how* they'd like to hear it.

If you're writing your landing pages with your prospect top-of-mind, they'll notice. And they'll thank you with a conversion.

And *that's* what conversion-centered copywriting is all about.

Five Content Writing Tips That Will Automatically Make You a Better Blogger

In today's digital world, blogging is an important piece of the marketing pie. By minimizing its importance, you're throwing away an opportunity to get your business some much-needed exposure.

Many business owners choose not to blog because they think they don't have the skills to write engaging content. But you don't need to be a writing expert to blog. You just need a few tips to help you along.

Here are five writing tips that'll automatically make you a better blogger and (hopefully) generate traffic to your site.

1. Use the AIDA formula

Many copywriters use a formula called AIDA to help with sales and marketing copy. You can apply the same formula to your blog posts. So, what is AIDA?

- **Attention:** You can grab your readers attention by writing a powerful headline. Write something that piques their curiosity.

- **Interest:** You can engage your audience by telling a short story. It doesn't have to be anything elaborate, just something that will create a hook.

- **Desire:** Create desire. One way is to allude to something that will be happening in the near future. People are curious by nature.

- **Action:** Tell your readers what you want them to do.

2. Don't write for search engines

A long, long time ago, stuffing your blog posts with keywords would help attract more traffic to your site.

Today's reality is that the value that the content provides for an audience is more important.

Sure, it doesn't hurt to have a strategically placed keyword in your headline or your title tags, but your content should always reflect your target audience's interests.

3. Use the word 'you'

It's been said that "you" is the most important word in content writing. People want solutions to their problems. You'll need to demonstrate how your product or service can help them. If you make it about them, they'll take notice. A good idea would be to use "you" in the opening sentence. That way, you have the reader's attention from the get-go.

Just a word of caution, though: Don't use the word "you" just for the sake of using it. First, you'll need to understand your audience. What will resonate with them? What do they want to know about? Doing your homework first will give you an advantage and help you create a connection.

4. Be conversational

Write like you talk—but just a little more polished. Trying to sound technical won't impress your audience. In fact, they'll be more likely to click away from your page. They want to read posts they can relate to. A conversational tone makes your audience feel you are talking to them, rather than at them. It makes them feel like they are being engaged in a conversation.

If you can make them feel a part of your story, then you'll have automatic fans.

Don't focus so much on your writing skills, per say. That's what an editor is for. Being engaging is far more important.

5. Use the KISS principle

Last but not least, always remember the KISS principle. It stands for "keep it simple, stupid." You don't need to complicate things. Keep it short, sweet, to the point. Your readers are busy people, so they appreciate content they can quickly read, chew on, and absorb.

Chew on this food for thought

There are hundreds of millions of blogs. How can you carve out a place for yourself without drowning in the sea full of competitors? Quality!

By creating high-quality content that people want to read, you can separate yourself from the rest. Sure, there's more to it than that, but before you can even consider the next steps, you have to ensure that what you write is engaging.

People have very short attention spans. People generally won't spend more than 20 seconds on your site before deciding whether it's worth their time. Keep that in mind when writing your next post.

Now that you have some tips on writing better content for your blog, you need to implement them. No one says you have to blog daily (although the more you do it, the better you'll get at it). You just need to start and be consistent. Find a schedule that works for you. Once you get in a groove, you'll start to see benefits.

The Benefits of Byline Authorship, and How to Do It Right

When a business owner decides to dip a toe into the waters of marketing, the choices can seem overwhelming. Should she buy a few ads? Sponsor some events? Put out a few press releases?

Short of jumping all the way in with a full-fledged marketing plan, entrepreneurs can start with one tactic that is inexpensive and pays big dividends: content marketing in the form of bylined articles, or article marketing.

Today's media landscape is not the closed-door fortress it once was. True, traditional media relations still hinge on convincing the right reporter or editor that your story is worth telling. However, many publications and online outlets are hungry for content written by guest bloggers or authors. At a time when media are short-staffed, highly competitive, and niche oriented, subject-matter experts have an opportunity to talk directly to readers.

When you get such an opportunity, use it to solve a customer problem, shape a market conversation, clarify a confusing issue, or introduce a new concept. Contributing content isn't about direct sales; it's about positioning yourself, your colleagues, and your business as industry thought leaders.

The benefits of getting this high-value tactic right are many. You'll gain authority in your market, you'll improve your search engine optimization (SEO), and you'll spark conversations that can generate leads.

Follow the following three steps to get started.

Write articles that humans would want to read

You have two elements to consider: First, you have to come up with some ideas that appeal to your target market. Second, you have to write for real readers, not search engines.

Let's start with the first issue: What can you write about? Begin with your audience in mind. The most-read articles are those that solve problems for their readers: "Five Steps for Building an At-Home Aquarium," "How to Save Money on Your Energy Bill," "Get Ready for the Next Big Threat to Data Security."

You are an expert in your industry, you know what keeps your prospects up at night, and your articles should speak to those topics.

If you're starting from scratch, brainstorm a list of possible topics, and then see whether they pass the "so what?" test. Would those topics matter in five years? Who would care about them today? Whittle down your list of potential topics by asking those questions of each one and crossing off any with unsatisfactory responses.

Chances are, though, that you're not starting from scratch. You can repurpose existing content into polished articles. Repurposing isn't about plagiarizing yourself: No one wants to read a cut-and-pasted brochure in the pages of his favorite magazine; moreover, such an approach will actually hurt your SEO efforts (and your credibility). However, you can mine what you've already written for good ideas, which can then be rewritten as fresh material.

Start by looking at what you already have:

- Whitepapers
- Survey results
- Infographics
- Presentations
- Blog posts
- Webinar content
- Case studies

Now that you have your ideas and some source content, it's time to write. Again, remember your audience. Your readers don't need a hard-sell; they need information. Give it to them as straightforwardly as you can, and avoid some of the most common sins of marketing writing, including these:

- Relying on jargon

- Flouting the rules of grammar

- Ignoring the reader's interest

- Burying the "so what?"

- Taking liberties with the truth

- Baiting search engines

Good article marketing (like good writing) starts with getting real—and telling a story that matters to the reader (the human one, not the search bot).

Craft a compelling pitch and target it to the right publication

Your media targets will differ, depending on the audiences you want to reach and the story you want to tell with a particular pitch. Keep the story angle in mind, and then determine your local print, Web, and broadcast targets, as well as vertical and national publications and any other applicable outlets.

For example, if you run a Boston-based bicycle business, your audience is local cyclists or physically active residents. Your publication targets would include local blogs, Boston-based business publications, cycling magazines, and similar outlets.

Craft a pitch with a particular publication in mind. The one or two paragraph article overview you send should reflect your knowledge of the publication's audience and the interests of the editor you're contacting. Make sure your pitch is brief, illustrative of your market knowledge, relevant to the publication and its audience, and timely.

When you capture the interest of a publication or online outlet, make it easy for the editor or publisher to work with you. Be transparent and authentic. Follow the publication's writing guidelines, and meet your deadlines.

Distribute your published article and encourage readers to share it via social media

Congratulations! Your article has appeared in a publication that your customers, prospects, partners, and investors read. But your work isn't done yet.

The beauty of byline articles and guest blogs posts is that the output has greater reach than just the single publication in which it appears. Share the link to the article on your social media platforms: Twitter, Facebook, Google+, LinkedIn. Write about it on your company's blog and share it in any e-newsletters you put out.

Whether readers see your article when it's originally published or find it via your post-publication distribution, if the content strikes a chord—and it should if you crafted it well—readers will want to share it. And then it's up to you to convert your writing success into leads.

As readers move from your article to your company's website, make sure they can find more helpful content when they get there. Offer a free download of an e-book, a newsletter subscription, or a reservation for an upcoming webinar. Cultivate your new leads, and prepare your next article pitch to keep your momentum high.

Lessons From the Greatest Marketer of All Time...Expelled From Oxford

The marketer in question is, of course, David Ogilvy. He was given the educational opportunity of a lifetime—the chance to study at the prestigious University of Oxford. He was expelled, with the reason undisclosed, in 1931.

Ogilvy never had a college degree, proving you don't need to have a marketing degree to be a fantastic marketer. However, the experiences in the years that followed did shape him into one of the greatest marketers ever.

The Wilderness Years

After a brief stint as a kitchen monkey in a Paris hotel, Ogilvy started working for the Aga Cookers company in England, selling stoves door to door. It was his first taste of marketing, and he excelled, eventually writing a sales manual for Aga salesmen described by Forbes as "probably the best sales manual ever written."

After fortuitously landing a job at a London agency in part because of that very manual, in 1938 Ogilvy was sent, at his request, to the United States to attend George Gallup's Audience Research Institute in New Jersey. He cited this experience as a huge influence on his thinking, because he learned not only research methods but also how to apply findings to real life.

In the 10 years that followed, Ogilvy worked for British Intelligence during the World War. He purchased farmland in rural Pennsylvania, where he lived among the Amish. By 1948 he realized that farming wasn't his calling, and he moved to New York to start his own ad agency.

Founding an Agency

Ogilvy became a founding member of Hewitt, Ogilvy, Benson & Mather (which would eventually become Ogilvy & Mather Worldwide), even though he had little experience as an ad man.

But after writing ads for such companies as Lever Brothers, General Foods, American Express, and Shell, Ogilvy soon became one of the most prominent figures in the world of advertising. Ogilvy on his successful ad copy: "They made Ogilvy & Mather so hot that getting clients was like shooting fish in a barrel."

Five of Ogilvy's Most Important Marketing Lessons

1. "Unless your advertising contains a big idea, it will pass like a ship in the night. I doubt if more than one campaign in a hundred contains a big idea."

If a marketing campaign is unsuccessful, it's likely because it lacks ambition and creativity. Ogilvy's thinking was that in a world of average you needed to cut through mediocrity with a big idea that captured people's attention.

Don't confuse the notion of a big idea with the loudest or most controversial idea, however; a big idea means seeing something no one else doing yet being brave enough to do it yourself. It's not about creating a wacky idea, but it is about doing something different and making it successful.

2. "In the modern world of business, it is useless to be a creative, original thinker unless you can also sell what you create."

This lesson may seem to contradict the first lesson, but the point is that you should never be creative merely for the sake of being creative; you should only be creative to achieve the most important thing as a marketer: sales.

Moreover, creativity does not automatically equate to better sales; how you apply that creativity is most important.

3. "I abhor advertising that is blatant, dull, or dishonest. Agencies which transgress this principle are not widely respected."

A lot of people will ponder whether this is a marketing lesson or a moral lesson. It definitely has elements of both. First, Ogilvy wanted his ads to carry integrity; he wasn't looking for short-term exposure that would lead to long-term pain either for his clients or his agency.

Whether it was a legacy or reputation that Ogilvy was trying to build, he wanted to create ad copy that would be respected and admired for a hundred years; he always had branding and his own image in mind.

4. "Advertising people who ignore research are as dangerous as generals who ignore decodes of enemy signals."

Ogilvy was not a marketer who trusted his success to luck; he did not base his ideas on gut feeling or random thought. He was scrupulous and thorough in his research, which he would use to ensure his ads reached and convinced their audiences.

After attending George Gallup's Audience Research Institute, he became a stickler for research and testing. It was not good enough for an ad to be successful; he had to know exactly why it was successful so he could take note for other ads.

5. "If we hire people who are smaller than we are, we will become a company of dwarfs. If we hire people who are larger than we are, we'll become a company of giants."

This is another lesson that epitomizes Ogilvy. He was not ego-driven; he didn't want to build an advertising agency with zealots, followers, and supporters. He wanted to hire people with the values he shared, but they had to be as good or better than those already working for him.

He was a huge believer in the value of community within a company; he was unreserved in his desire to help his employees and ensure their happiness (both at work and at home), believing that a happy worker was a good worker, in the simplest terms.

But Ogilvy wasn't soft. In giving everything to his employees, he expected the same back in their work. His ethos was, If I give you the resources and help, to be a giant in marketing, then you had better show me you're a giant. There was no sentimentality.

Writing and Readability Scores: It Matters

Creating high-quality content is more important than it's ever been, thanks in part to the recent infamous algorithm updates by Google.

Now, when creating a blog post, article, or any other written content, you must make sure that it's not only highly relevant to your audience but also specifically tailored for them—its language, in particular.

For example, if you're creating a post for a site that gives advice to parents, the post is naturally going to be a lot less formal than if you're creating a post that sets out analyst forecasts and discusses them. The language that you use will be different, as will the readability factor. Before you begin writing, then, it pays to know your audience.

Some Best-Practices for Writing for the Web

Writing for the Web uses skills, language, and design elements that are different from those used for print. Before we discuss readability, let's have a look at a few of the basics of text for the Web:

1. You should use white space. Keep paragraphs short, no more than six lines, and ensure there is clear white space between each.
2. Use shorter words and sentences, depending on your target audience.
3. Use language that is known to the target audience. When writing for technology or corporate markets, for example, some jargon might be necessary.

Flesch-Kincaid Readability Scoring

Flesch-Kincaid was developed by Austrian-born Rudolf Flesch, who fled to the US to avoid the Nazi invasion. He was a readability expert who studied law in his home country before going on to graduate from Columbia University with a PhD in English.

Flesch was also a writing consultant and created the Flesch Reading Ease test, and he was the co-creator of the Flesch-Kincaid readability test. He was one of the earliest proponents of writing in plain English.

According to Flesch, the formula for readability that he devised works because it is "based on some very complicated facts of human psychology. It works because it is based on the way the human mind works."

When someone is reading, the mind and eyes focus on "successive points," allowing for a tentative judgment to be made in the mind of the reader as to what the text means up to that point. Natural breaks in the text, such as punctuation marks or new paragraphs, allow the mind to re-evaluate the text up to the point, when the mind stops for a split second, until it eventually arrives at the final meaning.

The longer the word, sentence, or paragraph, the longer the brain has to suspend comprehending ideas until it can reach a point where all of the words make sense together.

Because they require more mental work by the reader, longer words and sentences are harder to read and understand.

The Flesch-Kincaid formula requires you to count words and syllables in order to measure the amount of mental work that may be required by the reader. On a scale of 0 to 100, 0 is measured as the most difficult, 100 the easiest.

To use the formula, count the length of each of the following:

- Words
- Syllables

- Sentence up to where they are marked by a full stop, colon, semicolon, dash, question mark, or exclamation point

Then divide the average number of syllables per word, words per sentence, and average sentence length, and score using the following image:

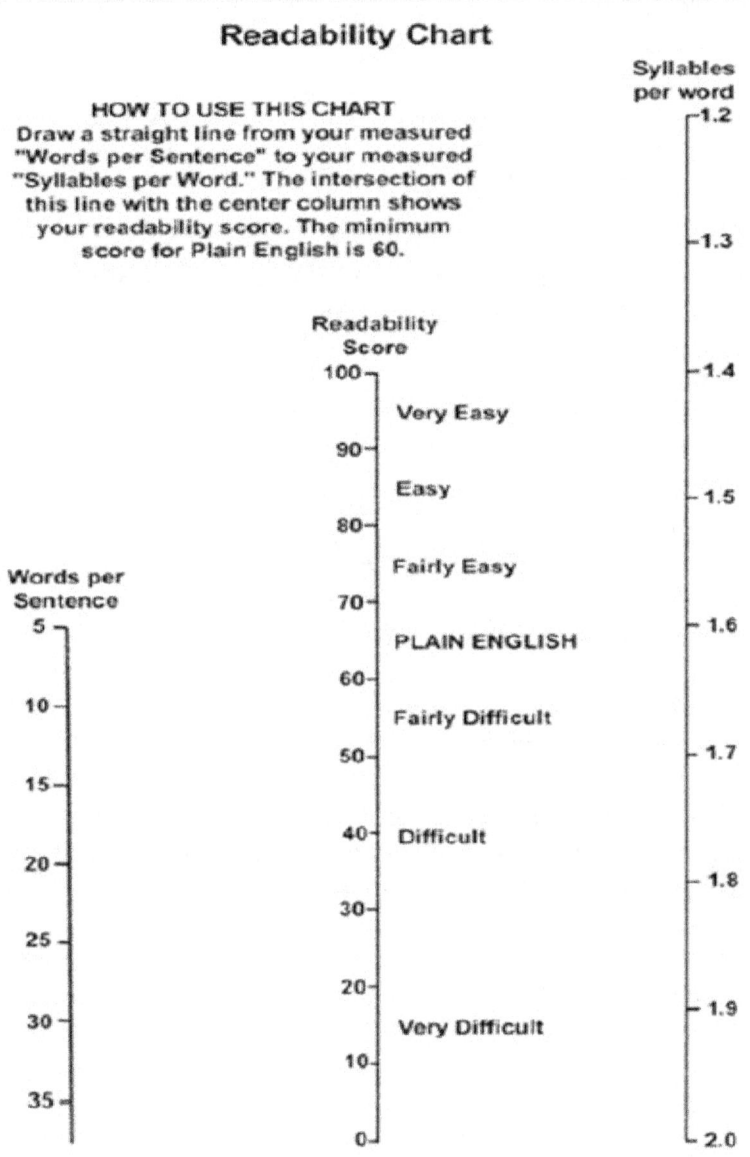

You can work out the readability score by taking a ruler and connecting the two figures that you have for sentence and word length; where the line crosses the figure in the center column is your readability score.

Using the Formula

$$206.835 - 1.015 \left(\frac{\text{total words}}{\text{total sentences}} \right) - 84.6 \left(\frac{\text{total syllables}}{\text{total words}} \right)$$

So, multiply the average sentence length by 1.015, average word length by 84.6, add the two numbers, and then subtract that total from 206.835 to arrive at the readability score.

If a text's readability score is...

- 90.0-100.0, it easily understood by an average 11-year-old student

- 60.0-70.0, it is easily understood by 13-15-yearold Students

- 0.0-30.0, it is best understood by university graduates

You may think that you're insulting your readership by sticking to a score of around 60, but you're not; you're just writing in plain, understandable English.

When we read on a monitor, we don't behave in the same way as when we're reading a book or magazine. We tend to scan a lot more, so shorter words and sentences become even more important.

Flesch recommends that the score of the average conversational piece aimed at consumers be a minimum of 80 (approximately 15 words per sentence and 1-1.5 syllables per word).

Examples of average scores for various types of content:

- Comics: 92
- Consumer advertisements: 82
- Reader's Digest: 65
- Time magazine: 52
- Harvard Business Review: 43
- Standard insurance policy: 10

As you can see, the scores differ according to the target audience. Harvard Business Review assumes a readership with a certain level of education. An insurance policy will include a lot of industry-relevant language and so has a very low readability score.

Determining Readability in MS Word

Microsoft Office products include a readability scoring tool based on the Flesch-Kincaid formula. To enable it in Word...

Go to Options > choose Proofing > ensure that the grammar with spelling box is checked > select the tick box for Show readability statistics.

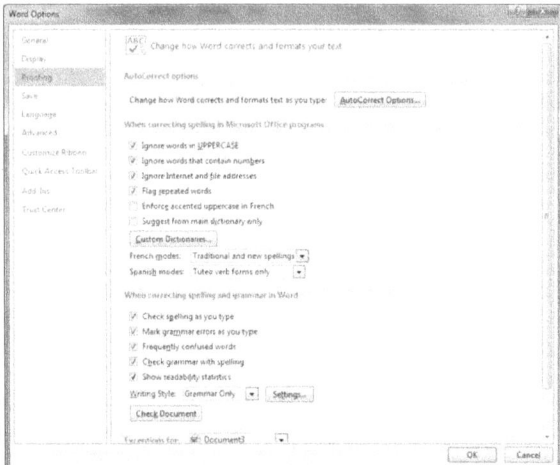

When checking the document for spelling and grammar, you will see a box displaying statistics and scores.

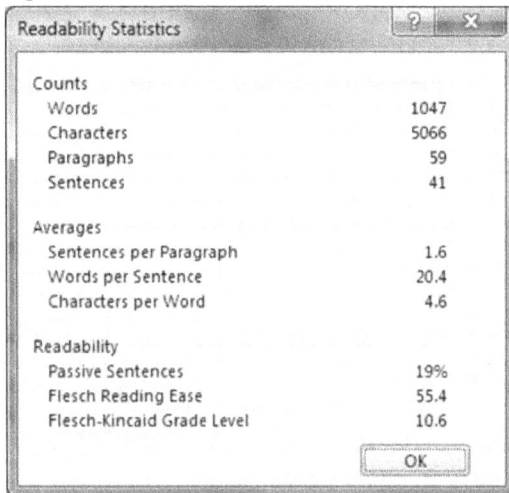

Troubleshooting

If you've finished your post only to find it has a readability score of 20, say, you can address the issue during editing. Consider breaking up long sentences into one or more smaller sentences, and cut out words of over three syllables

Flesch maintained that there are no complex, legalistic words that can't be translated into plain English. In Word, use the synonym function to help you choose similar words if you get stuck. You can do this by right-clicking on the offending word and choosing a synonym; Word will bring up a list of alternatives. For example:

- Intricate
- Complex
- Complicated
- Longwinded
- Long-winded
- Elaborate
- Difficult
- Tortuous
- Thesaurus...

That was the list of words given as alternatives to the word "convoluted"; as you can see, you have the further option of using the Thesaurus should you still be stuck for a better word.

It's also a good idea to use contractions such as don't and they're. Another idea is to use two-word combinations such as on-site instead of at the customer's workplace.

In short, the key to authoring good content is to use language that doesn't detract from your message.

Five Incredibly Specific Tactics for Writing Enchanting Copy

Let's imagine for a moment that someone lands on your website. Not just *any* someone—but a dream client-type someone. This person would be amazing to work with, and (at this moment) it's all up to your website to reel 'em in.

This person starts reading your copy and the words are jumping out at him.

He is thinking to himself: "This person gets me."

He reads on and is so enchanted by the story you are telling that he clicks over to your services page. Things keep getting better, because your service descriptions are so spot-on, he immediately feels the desire to trade his cold hard cash for the chance to work with you.

Sound too good to be true? *It doesn't have to be.*

The Web is chock-full of boring copy. But your website doesn't need to mingle with that group.

Creating copy that connects with your audience is easier than you think. But it's not enough to just "talk benefits" and "use your own voice" (and other such vague advice you've likely run across).

Instead, you need ultra-specific tactics that you can put to use on your own website. Here is a list of five such tactics (plus a bonus if you read until the end. Yes, that's a bribe).

1. Branded statements

Have you run across businesses or entrepreneurs that have perfect snippets of advice they use over and over again to sum up the core of their brand or philosophy?

These people are onto something.

Repetition is known to be effective, and there is a way to put it to use in your copy to enchant your audience and help them remember you long after they've wondered away from your site.

I like to call that little trick "branded statements."

How to do it:
What do you believe about your industry or niche that makes you unique? What piece of break-through advice do you love to offer your clients or customers?

Once you find a nugget or two of wisdom or wit that's uniquely you (it might take some brainstorming), you have the basis for your very own branded statements.

Condense that piece of advice or insight into a short sentence or two. Word it in a conversational way (so it doesn't sound awkward or scripted when spoken out loud). Memorize it.

Whenever relevant, use your branded statements on your website. And here's a bonus: Use it in guest posts or during interviews to help build brand awareness online.

Remember to use it often: The power of branded statements is in repetition.

2. Use fragments
Grammatically correct copy can be awful to read.

Don't get me wrong, structure and rules are important. But if you stick to them too religiously, your copy runs the risk of turning out so uptight that your audience will avoid it at all cost.

When we talk out loud, in conversation, we tend to communicate in a more casual way—and it turns out that this way of talking translates well onto the Web.

One super-effective way to break up with traditional grammar is by deploying the sentence fragment. This little guy breaks up the monotony of your copy and helps emphasize important points. Plus, it's just plain fun to use (and read) for some reason.

How to do it:
A sentence fragment just means you've cut a sentence short. Like this. It doesn't include all the elements of a proper sentence—which is exactly why it works. It stands out. Grabs attention.

Use sentence fragments sparingly (they can get annoying if you go overboard). Put them to use when you need to break up the flow of a paragraph or create an abrupt rhythm, or when you want to emphasize a point.

3. Show vulnerability

We all go to great lengths to hide our shortcomings and weaknesses. But it turns out that when you show vulnerability, you can actually endear yourself to your audience.

People want to make a human connection, even on the Internet. And hiding behind a perfectly polished persona doesn't make you seem human.

Showing vulnerability allows your audience to relate with you. More important, when you've overcome (or you admit to trying to overcome) something (a problem, a shortcoming) that your audience desperately wants to overcome as well, they grow to trust you, which in turn increases your authoritative online presence.

How to do it:
What have you struggled with that your audience struggles with as well? What past experiences have you had that makes your work close to your heart?

Showing vulnerability is as simple as incorporating those types of stories into your copy.

But this one comes with a caveat: You need to be super extra careful to avoid TMI (too much information) syndrome. People don't want to hear about your problems unless it relates to them.

So be strategic with your vulnerability and make sure it serves a purpose and offers value.

4. Steal words

Want to know the real-deal secret to enchanting copy? The secret that even top-paid copywriters use?

It has absolutely nothing to do with coming up with your own perfect words. It's all about hunting down the words your dream clients and customers are already using, and snagging them for use in your own content.

Your audience is busy expressing themselves all over the Web—using words, phrases, and ideas that, when transplanted into your own copy, will make your audience feel right at home (and completely understood).

How to do it:

This is probably the most effective way to make your copy memorable, relatable, and completely non-ignorable (I made up that word. See tip No. 2 about breaking grammar rules).

But it also happens to be one of the simplest. It doesn't require wordsmithing on your part, since your audience will be doing most of the heavy lifting for you.

All you need to do is listen in on what your audience is saying. Using social media is a great place to start. Check on Twitter, Facebook, and Google+. Hit up popular blogs that attract your dream customers and sift through the comments.

You're looking for a few specific things:

- How do your prospects express themselves? (Do they use a lot of slang? Are they into polished, professional prose?)

- What specific words do they use to describe the type of service or product you offer?

- How do they express their fears, concerns, and desires related to your offering?

Once you've gathered some from-the-trenches verbiage, infuse that language into your own copy.

Bam! *Irresistibility.*

5. Get visual

I know we're talking copy, and photography and design are so another topic. But hear me out.

Creating enchanting copy basically comes down to connection. You have to have a connection with your reader. Part of building that connection in the online world is presenting yourself visually.

When you use actual images of yourself, your readers can picture your actual person while hearing your voice in your copy—which makes their experience more personal.

How to do it:
Just as your copy should be uniquely you and should represent your brand story, your visuals should be unique as well. There's no need to pose for a buttoned-up, traditional headshot. Be yourself. Represent the type of brand you're building.

Whether you hire a professional or enlist the help of nothing but a tripod and self-timer, let your personality come through in your photos and give your audience a real preview of the person they are listening to.

Now it's your turn

A lot of tips for creating enchanting copy just didn't make it into this post (space issues and all that). One of the finalists that didn't make the cut was **interaction**.

Your copy shouldn't be a one-way expression. It should get your audience involved. And the same applies to this article.

So now it's your turn to weigh in. What makes you sit up and pay attention to some bits of copy and not others? What brands or businesses have you completely in love with their online voice?

Five Tips to Enhance Your Call to Action

Think of the last time you responded to a marketing communication. What made you do it? Was there an incentive, or a chance to win something? A good call to action (CTA) is a lot more than just a link. Very rarely will you get someone to follow your call to action by simply asking them.

In nearly 10 years of working with direct mail, I've found a few tips you can use to enhance your calls to action and get people to respond.

1. Use a Widget

In the marketing world, a unique element makes your message stand out among the other messages in the same medium. If we're talking direct mail, a widget means something that isn't paper. In the past, I have used car keys, credit cards, and casino chips. They add physical weight to the mailer and help it stand out from other items in a mailbox. It draws attention to the message, and it gets the recipient to engage.

Widgets work online, too. Rather than a standard lead-capture form, add an interactive game, well designed imagery, or even unique colors to make your communication stand out. The ultimate goal is to make it look different from your competitors' marketing and keep the consumer's attention long enough to take the desired action.

2. Offer Prizes

I believe in the idea of reciprocity. When you are looking to drive engagement, offering prizes is a great solution. If you give consumers something for engaging with you, they are more likely to return the favor. For example, if you won a TV at a furniture store, where are you most likely to go when it is time to buy your next couch or bedroom set? Part of human nature is that we tend to take care of each other. When someone does something for us, we reciprocate.

Offering prizes of some kind—like popular gift cards—can help you build a relationship with a consumer beyond just the CTA. Of course, you don't simply want to pay your consumers to interact with you. Put some thought into the prize and make sure you're still going to earn ROI on your marketing. If nothing else, give them an opportunity to win a prize: "For responding, your name will be entered to win a $100 gift card!"

3. Personalization

We all love to feel special. Personalizing your CTA tells consumers you understand that they are unique. Add a handwritten sticky note, use their name in your greeting, or personalize offers to match their lifestyle.

For online use, create a landing page that recognizes the visitor and pre-populates the information you already know about them. Doing so also increases the ease of use by allowing them to quickly complete forms.

Another good method of personalization is speaking about something you know they already own— whether a car, television, or a tanning package. Doing so can tell them this isn't just mass marketing, you're thinking about them as individuals.

4. Clarity of Intent

This one can't be overstated, and it works the same for both print and online: Your CTA has to be clear. There's no room for vagueness in a CTA. Make the next step obvious, and give a specific time frame for completion. Does the offer expire in an hour? Tell them that. Have every incentive driver point to one location—the CTA—and be clear about what steps should be taken.

5. Repetition

Within your messaging, whether direct mail, email, or a newspaper ad, zero in on exactly what you're trying to accomplish and state that message. Be clear, and repeat the message. People are more likely to remember something—as well as take action—if they're presented with the option multiple times.

This works in two ways. First, within a specific marketing communication, make sure that your CTA is called out multiple times throughout the piece. Second, try multiple marketing mediums. For example, don't stop at just a TV commercial. Try the same promotion in a print ad or email campaign.

Whether you use the same medium multiple times or you track across multiple media, repeating yourself can help increase the impact of your message.

* * *

Whatever your company is doing, make absolutely sure that you're tracking the results. Marketing isn't one size fits all. If you're going to try something new, A/B-test it. At the very least, test the idea against similar campaigns you've done in the past. Pick one variable to change and track how it impacts the results. If it works, great! If it doesn't work, adjust and try something else.

Targeting the right consumer can affects your results as well. Know your target, find a group, and go after them. If you're tracking correctly, you'll see remarkable results.

Five Surprising Ways to Write Addictive Business Blog Posts

It's so frustrating: You work hard running your business. You know your industry inside and out. You offer something that nobody else does. And you take precious time to write about it in your business blog. Yet... nobody is reading. Your social share buttons are untouched. And your comment sections are empty too.

And you're definitely not getting more phone calls or walk-in traffic to justify the time you've invested in writing a new post week after annoying week.

So, why isn't your blog getting the attention it deserves? You know people are looking for the expertise and answers you provide. What are you missing?

You're probably missing something all successful bloggers know how to do: write engaging content. Content so insightful and useful that readers become addicted. Hooked.

You, too, can write engaging content. You just need to make a few adjustments to your writing.

Use the following five methods to write a business blog that totally hooks your readers.

1. Write with all five senses

Include sight, sound, smell, taste, and touch. Being factual in a business blog is important, but you can present your information in an appealing way. Immerse your reader, make him smell something stinky or hear something that makes him flinch. We are sensory beings. We respond to and remember writing that makes us feel something.

Try this: Trying to gain traction as a blogger can feel like climbing a hill that gets steeper and longer with every step.

Instead of this: It is difficult to write a blog, and also to find readers.

We know what it feels like to climb a hill. It's exhausting. And that feeling immediately gives your reader a sense of the difficulty you're referring to.

2. Get to the point

Start your post with a strong lead. Your reader wants to know whether you understand her needs and will give her the solutions she's looking for. She won't stick around if you start with paragraphs of background information.

Get her hooked right away. She's coming to you for her hit, and she'll get it from someone else if you don't grab her attention.

Try this: Wearing sunscreen will prevent sunburns now and wrinkles in the future.

Instead of this: Sunscreen was first introduced in the 1920s and has undergone many different formulations in the past 95 years. Let's go through all of them.

When you show your reader that you understand her concerns right from the start, she'll want to keep reading.

3. Ignore your English teacher

Mrs. Kelly, my fourth grade English teacher, insisted on formal compositions that had little or no dialogue. That requirement shocked my nine-year-old self. Dialogue was what I most enjoyed.

Looking back now, I know that Mrs. Kelly was encouraging logical transitions and grammatically correct writing.

And those are important.

But they can also make for boring writing that doesn't create a relationship with your reader. You don't have to include dialogue, but you should write like you speak. That means you should vary sentence length, end a sentence with a preposition, or start a sentence with "and" or "but."

Mrs. Kelly would not approve.

Try this: We help you build your business with comprehensive and long-term advice from experienced team members. Our team members have skills. And they're specialized.

Instead of this: The accomplished accountants at Grey, Timeworn and Musty have had decades of experience providing information about reporting requirements, reorganizing tax structures and performing valuations that are achieved using financial and economic information that use quantifiable calculations and tools.

People want to do business with people, not with a company. And when you write like you speak, it sounds approachable, human, interesting.

4. Embarrass yourself

Don't be shy. Put yourself out there by revealing your mistakes. It's more human, and people will remember and identify with what you're saying.

Write like nobody's reading. (Sadly, for most of us, that won't be hard to imagine.)

People love to read something interesting and relatable: So tell me something that went horribly wrong or about a terrible mistake you made. It would be like an accident on the highway. People can't look away.

Try this: When I quit my job to start my business, I told my boss that I never wanted to work for anybody again. Especially a jerk like him.

Instead of this: I made a lot of mistakes when I first started out, but with hard work I am a success today.

When you tell a true story that reveals a weakness or misstep, it creates a connection with your reader. We can empathize because we all blunder at times.

5. Don't be a show-off

Your mom was right. About everything. But especially about nobody liking a show-off.

Show us that you know your stuff, but don't try to impress us with your big, meaningless words. Impress us by using language that is direct and simple.

When you show off with big words and jargon, you put a barrier between us. Or worse: You make us feel dumb. And will we come back to your blog only to feel dumb? Not likely.

Try this: Modern teachers know that students are excited to learn when they are engaged.

Instead of this: 21st-century pedagogy requires a paradigm shift to facilitate student inquiry.

Show us your expertise with clear and concise writing. We want to learn from you, but when you use unfamiliar jargon… you prevent us from learning.

Give your readers their fix

These tips are simple. Just five easy writing tweaks that can transform your posts from forgettable to can't-live-without.

Because you don't want to have just another business blog. You want to write the best business blog in your industry.

And you can do it.

You already have the business expertise and experience. And now you have some specific advice and examples to improve your writing—to make your posts addictive.

So give it a try. Hook your readers and satisfy their cravings. They won't be able to stop themselves from coming back for more.

This Writing GPS Helps You Create Ridiculously Good Content

The writer Andre Dubus (*House of Sand and Fog*) has described writing as inching your way along a very dark, very long tunnel: You can make out the next few feet in front of you, but you're not quite certain where you'll end up or when you'll get there.

For me, at times, writing can feel like birthing a Volkswagen. What helps with the uncertainty and enormity of the task is to start with some kind of process to guide the way—necessary checkpoints toward that final piece or the beacons that guide the entire effort.

Process is one of those things that in many parts of life I consider hopelessly boring and mind-numbing. Like peeling the skins of raw tomatoes—or scrubbing dirt from beets.

But in writing, process is necessary because you need a road map to get you to where you need to be—essentially, a kind of writing GPS that gets you from discombobulated thoughts to a coherent, cogent piece of writing that others can understand and appreciate.

Though there is no one way to write—just as there is no one way to roast a turkey or parent a child—there are terrible ways to do all three.

What works for me is the process I outline here. Maybe it will inspire you, too. In any event, I suggest you find some process: Good writing takes planning and preparation; it doesn't just emerge, fully formed, as if from the head of Zeus. Or your own head, for that matter.

What follows is an outline of a 12-step process for relatively long text you might produce—blog posts, e-books, whitepapers, site content, and the like. It's the process I use to write any post and book. Also, I've used it to cobble together the bones of video scripts and presentations, as well as longer memo style emails.

Here's the CliffsNotes of it.

1. Goal.

What's your business goal? What are you trying to achieve?

Anything you write—even an individual blog post— should be aligned with a larger (business or marketing) goal.

The key here is that you care about what you're writing: You can try to fake it, but your readers will be allergic to your insincerity. Why does that matter? Because if you don't care about what you're writing about, no one will.

Let's say your goal is this: *I want to drive awareness of and interest in the launch of our incredibly cool new collaborative editing software because we want to sell more of it.*

2. Reframe.

Put your reader into it.

Reframe the idea to relate it to your readers. Why does it matter to them? What's in it for them? Why should they care? What's the clear lesson or message you want them to take away? What value do you offer them? What questions might they have? What advice or help can you provide?

My friend Tim Washer of Cisco refers to this reframing as giving your audience a gift: How can you best serve them, with a mind-set of generosity and giving?

To get to the heart of this reframing, I ask "So what?" and then answer, "Because..."

Repeat that "so what/because" query and response string as many times as necessary—until you've exhausted any ability to come up with an answer.

Or until you're questioning things best left to the philosophers.

As in...

I want to drive interest and awareness in the launch of our new collaborative editing software.

So what?

Because our new text editor makes it stupid-easy in three specific ways for those of you without a geek gene to easily collaborate from remote locales, without overwriting each other's stuff or losing earlier versions.

So what?

Because all that's a pain to deal with, and it causes a lot of frustration and suffering for collaborative, virtual teams.

So what?

Because pain... it hurts. And suffering is... umm... bad.

You get the idea.

Express your reframed idea as a clear message. In this case, something like this:

Our new text editor makes it stupid-easy in three specific ways for those of you without a geek gene to easily work together from remote locales, without overwriting each other's stuff or losing earlier versions, which makes for happier, less frustrated collaborators. You'll get your work done faster, with less wasted effort.

Then put that at the top of the page, like a bonfire on the beachhead, to remind you where you're headed with your writing.

3. Seek out the data and examples.

What credible source supports your main idea? Can you cite examples, data, real-world stories, relevant anecdotes, timely developments, or new stories?

Don't discount your own experience; at the same time, don't rely exclusively on it. Use yourself as one of your sources if you have relevant experience. That works, because "the more personal you are, the more universal you become," writes Chip Scanlan, Poynter.org's writing advice columnist.

"The writer who uses herself as a source and resource has the greatest chance of connecting with the largest audience," Chip points out. "[A]sk yourself: What do I think about this story? What do I know about it?"

You'll want to research your topic, of course. But "the smart writers I know start out by tapping into their own private stock first," Chip says.

In our example, ask: Is there research that quantifies the problem? Who else has dealt with catastrophes or successes? Could you talk to those people or organizations to get their firsthand horror stories and advice? Also, what's been your own experience?

4. Organize.

What structure helps communicate your point? Some options are a list, a how-to guide, a client narrative, a Q&A, a contrarian view, a skeptical approach, how-to, case study... and so on.

Organize the outline or general architecture that suits that type of story best.

5. Write to one person.

Imagine the one person you're helping with this piece of writing. And then write directly to that person (using *you*, as opposed to using *people* or *they*).

Connect your reader to the issue you're writing about (again, why does it matter to him or her?), perhaps by relaying a scenario or telling a story. Put your reader (or someone just like him or her) into your story right up front—because you want the reader to recognize and relate to an issue.

6. Produce The Ugly First Draft.

Producing The Ugly First Draft (TUFD) is basically where you show up and throw up. Write badly. Write as if no one will ever read it. (Stephen King calls this "writing with the door closed.")

Don't worry about grammar, complete sentences, or readability. Don't fret about spelling or usage. You'll tackle all that later. For now, just get that TUFD down.

By the way, this show-up-and-throw-up phase is often where many bloggers end the process. But you won't do that—because you have respect both for your writing and for your reader.

7. Walk away.

Walking away is self-explanatory. You don't need to actually go for a walk, of course. Just put some distance between your first draft and the second.

How much distance depends on you. I try to put a day between my own (usually spectacularly ugly!) TUFD and the next step, because that amount of time seems to let my thinking season and mature. I feel better prepared to slap those words around a little, willing them to take shape on the page.

I don't always have the luxury of that long a fermentation period—and if a piece is tied to a news story, you might not either. So work with what you've got. But at least try to get out of the building—maybe grab a coffee or a slice of pie or something.

8. Rewrite.

Shape that mess into something that a reader wants to read. In your head, swap places with your reader as you do so.

Rewriting is the thing that separates us from the chimps. Or, at least, capable writers from less capable ones.

9. Give it a great headline or title.

Spend as much time on the headline as you do on the writing itself. Respect the headline.

The headline is not the metaphorical cherry on top, the dot over the i, the cross on the t, the icing on the cake, or the finishing flourish. Today, especially, it's a key element of your post, article, or other piece of content. It tells the audience what you are going to deliver, how you're going to deliver it, and why they should keep reading.

So spend time with it, think on it, and figure out how to best use that valuable bit of text.

10. Have someone edit.

Ideally, the person who edits your piece will have a tight grip on grammar, usage, style, and punctuation. Like a bona fide editor.

11. One final look for readability.

Does your piece look inviting, alluring, easy to scan? With short paragraphs and bold subheads? Are your lists numbered or bulleted?

For the most part, chunky chunks of text feel impenetrable and don't convey energy and movement.

In other words, bulky text doesn't look like much fun to read. Your words look like they're huddled together for warmth and meaning, like some sort of content shanty-town.

12. Publish

but not without answering one more reader question: "What now?" Don't leave your readers just standing awkwardly in the middle of the dance floor after the music stops. What do you want them to do next?

Check out other resources?
Sign up to hear more?
Register for an event or a free trial? Buy something?

Consider the order of the steps in this outlined writing process merely a suggestion. You can toss them around and follow them in any order you wish—perhaps you like to barf up your first draft onto the page incoherently and then organize your writing into something more cogent.

That's fine; it's completely at your discretion. There is no one way to write, remember?

(The only order I wouldn't suggest is backwards. Because that's just a formula for ridiculously bad content.)